For the ones who were never freed.
—A. J.

To us.
Those who forget our past are doomed to repeat it.
—E. B. L.

SIMON & SCHUSTER BOOKS FOR YOUNG READERS
An imprint of Simon & Schuster Children's Publishing Division
1230 Avenue of the Americas, New York, New York 10020
Text copyright © 2014 by Angela Johnson
Illustrations copyright © 2014 by E. B. Lewis
All rights reserved, including the right of reproduction in whole or in part in any form.
SIMON & SCHUSTER BOOKS FOR YOUNG READERS is a trademark of Simon & Schuster, Inc.
For information about special discounts for bulk purchases,
please contact Simon & Schuster Special Sales at 1-866-506-1949 or business@simonandschuster.com.
The Simon & Schuster Speakers Bureau can bring authors to your live event. For more information or to book an event, contact
the Simon & Schuster Speakers Bureau at 1-866-248-3049 or visit our website at www.simonspeakers.com.
Book design by Laurent Linn
The text for this book is set in Diotima LT Std.
The illustrations for this book are rendered in watercolor on 300-pound Arches cold press paper.
Manufactured in the United States of America
0115 PCH
2 4 6 8 10 9 7 5 3
Library of Congress Cataloging-in-Publication Data
Johnson, Angela, 1961–
All different now : Juneteenth, the first day of freedom / Angela Johnson ; illustrated by E.B. Lewis. — First edition.
Summary: In 1865, members of a family start their day as slaves, working in a Texas cotton field, and end it celebrating their
freedom on what came to be known as Juneteenth.
ISBN 978-0-689-87376-8 (hardcover)
[1. Juneteenth—Fiction. 2. Slavery—Fiction. 3. African Americans—Fiction. 4. Family life—Texas—Fiction. 5. Texas—
History—1865–1950—Fiction.] I. Lewis, Earl B., illustrator. II. Title.
PZ7.J629All 2014
[E]—dc23
2011038273
ISBN 978-1-4814-0647-5 (eBook)

All Different Now

Juneteenth, the First Day of Freedom

———— ◆ ————

ANGELA JOHNSON

Illustrated by E. B. LEWIS

———— ◆ ————

SIMON & SCHUSTER BOOKS FOR YOUNG READERS

New York   London   Toronto   Sydney   New Delhi

A June morning breeze off the port blew the smell of honeysuckle

past the fields,

across the yard,

and into our room
to wake us.

And nobody knew,
as we
ate a little,
talked a little,
and headed to the fields
as the sun was rising,
that soon,
it would be all different.

Then we worked,

and worked,

and worked some more

under the hot Texas sun.
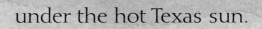

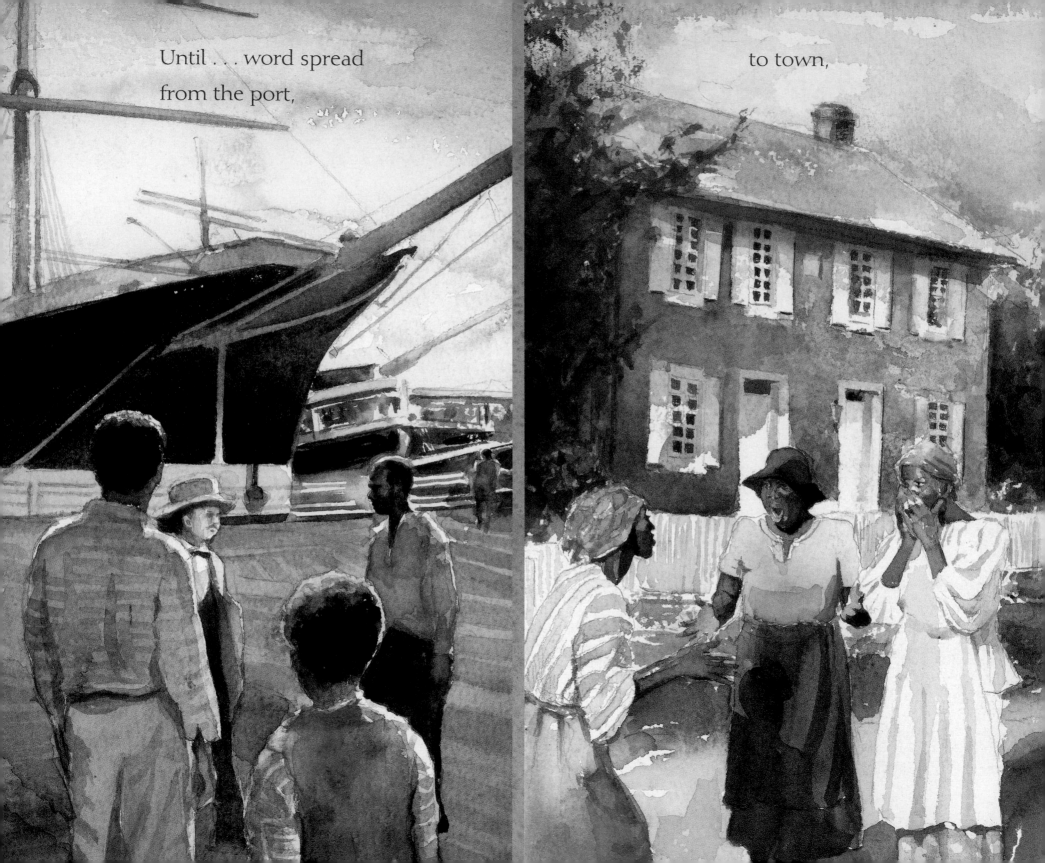

Until . . . word spread

from the port,

to town,

through the countryside,

and into the fields

that a Union general had read from a balcony that we were all

now and forever free

and things

would be

all different now.

I watched as my aunt Laura sang as she held her baby.
Mr. Jake, who some say was a hundred, cried quietly.

And a group of grown people bowed their heads
and whispered things to each other I could not hear.

My mama held my hand softly

and looked beyond,

as another breeze blew over

and everything

fell to a

hush.

But later . . .

Papa, Mama, the aunts and uncles, and all of
my cousins had an afternoon picnic by the water.
My baby brother crawled around our blanket as we
listened to the sounds of the waves.

And as more people joined us
we ate as a free people,
laughed as free people,
and told stories as free people
on
into
the night.

What was before

would be no more.

As we walked back home
the cool of the night
soothed our tired feet
that padded quietly past the shadowy
fields of cotton.

And in the morning
the smell of honeysuckle
will wake me again
beside my sisters and brother
to a time that will be,
for all of us,

all

different

now.

AUTHOR'S NOTE

As a small child visiting my grandmother's home in Alabama, I used to gaze enraptured at a large sepia photograph under a curved-glass frame of a woman in white sitting placidly in a chair with a tall, serious-looking man standing beside her. They were my grandmother's parents and they had been born slaves. At first, my great-grandparents were just long gone strangers who watched me through time. With every proceeding visit, though, I warmed to them and could not wait to curl up on my grandmother's flowered settee and stare back at them for hours.

They were a mystery, but tangible proof to my young eyes that all I'd learned about slavery in books was a reality in my own family.

Despite knowing a bit of my family history, I'd never really thought of their *moment* of emancipation. For some it did not come as early as it did for others.

A number of states (including Texas, where my story is set) had not returned to the Union by January 1, 1863, the date President Lincoln decreed the Emancipation Proclamation, so the slaves in those states didn't know they had been declared free. It was not until 1865 that the proclamation was finally decreed in Galveston, Texas.

Juneteenth, commemorated on June 19, is the celebration of that event, with Texas widely believed to be the first state to observe it. Today, more than forty states recognize Juneteenth in some way.

I'd love to know how my great-grandparents celebrated when told they were free. But that tale has been lost to time, so I can only hope that this one will do.

—ANGELA JOHNSON

ILLUSTRATOR'S NOTE

While trying to visually translate this beautifully poignant story by Angela Johnson, I found myself on a roller coaster of emotions, a ride that actually began several years earlier while reading Ralph Ellison's novel *Juneteenth*. This was my introduction to a piece of American history that inspired further research, so I viewed hundreds of old photographs and read many books on slavery. What I learned both enraged and thrilled me. I alternately felt despair and jubilation; grief in face of man's devastating inhumanity to man and joy for the resiliency and beauty of the human spirit.

I tried, over and over, to imagine what it must have been like to be a slave receiving the news of emancipation. To be given freedom for the first time in your life—wouldn't that be truly awesome, but also somehow surreal and dreamlike? I imagined that all things familiar and engrained must have suddenly seemed alien and strange. But all my attempts pointed to the same stark conclusion: It's simply impossible for a contemporary American, of any color, to put himself squarely in the shoes of a nineteenth-century slave.

This humbling moment of clarity made me realize that, although I've illustrated more than sixty books, this one would be my biggest challenge. It would stretch me the most. But at the same time Angela's manuscript lit me up like a light. What a fortuitous opportunity! It seemed our collaboration was predestined, and, as if to demonstrate this, everything I needed fell into place while my passion for the project blossomed.

To inspire my illustrations, I take reference photos that suggest the scenes of the book. This story required an enormous cast as well as costumes for all. And here I must gratefully acknowledge the people of Spartanburg County School District Seven in South Carolina. After a school visit I did there previously, I knew it was the perfect location for taking these photos. Just one phone call to Rodney Graves, director of secondary education, resulted in a wonderful and unexpected scene that brought me to tears. Arriving at a local park direct from the airport, I felt as though I'd walked into the nineteenth century. Students, teachers, parents, babies, preschoolers, grandparents, and even the superintendent were all dressed in clothing they had researched and provided themselves, ready to pose for their roles. After an entire day of photographing, the fun and easy part was done.

Now came the time to translate my experience into paint. The cumulative effect of all that I learned, including my reference photos, forced a wider view of this fateful event. So I tried to capture the whole mood of the day in shades of gray, rather than just black and white. Under a pale sky I illustrated not just jubilation and celebrations, but expressions of repose, disconnect, surprise, and contemplation.

I hope this book will act as a beacon that shines its light on a dark corner of our country's history and lays bare its collective denial. Once the darkness is illuminated, a deeper healing can occur and better assure our children's future. A future where all people wholeheartedly embrace and happily celebrate our differences.

—E. B. LEWIS

IMPORTANT DATES

January 1, 1863 President Abraham Lincoln issues the Emancipation Proclamation, which declares "that all persons held as slaves" within states that have seceded from the Union "are, and henceforward shall be, free." The proclamation makes freeing slaves the official end goal of the American Civil War, and allows African Americans to enlist in the Union army and navy. The Emancipation Proclamation does not end slavery in the United States, but it sets the stage for the constitutional amendment that will.

April 8, 1864 The Senate votes and agrees to add a thirteenth amendment to the United States Constitution. This thirteenth amendment will abolish slavery in every state.

January 31, 1865 The House of Representatives votes and agrees to add the Thirteenth Amendment to the Constitution, making slavery illegal in all states.

March 3, 1865 Congress creates the Bureau of Refugees, Freedmen, and Abandoned Lands to aid in the transition from slavery to freedom.

April 9, 1865 Confederacy General Robert E. Lee surrenders at the McLean House in the village of Appomattox Court House in Virginia. There were battles and skirmishes after this date, but it is generally considered the official end of the Civil War.

June 19, 1865 Major General Gordon Granger arrives in Galveston, Texas, with news that the Civil War has ended and all the slaves are free. During the war, Union soldiers could not get past the Confederate troops and enter Texas to tell the slaves about the Emancipation Proclamation. Then, when the war was over and slavery was officially illegal, plantation owners still did not tell their slaves that they were free. As a result, the slaves in Texas did not know that they were free until Major General Granger's announcement. This is why his arrival in Texas is known as the day that the last slaves were freed, and is celebrated as the first Juneteenth!

December 6, 1865 The Thirteenth Amendment is ratified by enough states and added to the Constitution.

At first Juneteenth was only celebrated within the African American community. Celebrators would play games, eat food, and dress in nice clothing to symbolize that they no longer wore the garments of slavery. Sometimes white landowners would oppose the celebration by refusing to let their newly freed workers use their property. In response, Juneteenth celebrations mostly took place at churches or on donated land. Eventually, in the 1890s, sites like Emancipation Park in Houston, Texas, and Booker T. Washington Park in Mexia, Texas, were bought specifically for holding Juneteenth celebrations.

During the early 1900s interest in celebrating Juneteenth declined. The Emancipation Proclamation was credited with ending slavery, and General Granger's role in freeing the Texas slaves two and half years after the proclamation was widely forgotten. Then, in the 1930s, the Great Depression forced many people off the farms and into the cities for jobs. Unless June 19 fell on a weekend, there were very few participants available to celebrate, as they had to go to work.

Awareness of Juneteenth increased again during the civil rights movement in the 1950s and 1960s. African Americans reconnected with this important part of their slave heritage and used it to fuel their fight for equal rights. The Poor People's March in Washington, DC, in 1968 especially inspired many African Americans to begin celebrating Juneteenth again. Throughout the next several years, African American state legislator Al Edwards helped to increase awareness of Juneteenth until it was finally declared an official state holiday in Texas on January 1, 1980.

In today's society Juneteenth is widely celebrated. It is a day for celebrating African American freedom and achievement. The Smithsonian, Henry Ford Museum, and countless other institutions sponsor activities and celebrations for Juneteenth, hoping to educate more people about African American history and culture in general. However, Juneteenth has also morphed into a more national, symbolic celebration of respect for all cultures.

ONLINE SOURCES

juneteenth.com

www.archives.gov

history.umd.edu/research/freedmen

memory.loc.gov

civilwar.org

juneteenthohio.net

ushistory.org

gettysburgcivilwar150.com

KEY TERMS

abolish: To put an end to. At the end of the Civil War, the American people abolished, or put an end to, slavery.

amendment: A change or alteration. When Congress passed the Thirteenth Amendment, they changed the Constitution so that all slaves were freed.

Civil War: In 1861, the American people argued about the problem of slavery. People in the Northern states wanted to get rid of slavery, while people in the Southern states wanted to keep slavery. The North and South could not peacefully work out their argument, so they began to fight. They fought for four years until the North won and slavery was abolished.

Confederacy: When the Southern states broke off from the North, they created their own government. This government was called the Confederacy. Soldiers from the Confederacy were known to wear gray uniforms during the Civil War.

constitution: A collection of laws. The United States has a constitution stating the laws that every citizen must follow.

ratify: To sign or give formal consent to. The individual states ratified the Thirteenth Amendment, making it officially valid.

secede: To formally withdraw from an official group. The Southern states seceded, or withdrew, their support from the United States. As a result, the United States broke into two parts called the Union and the Confederacy.

slavery: Slavery is when one person owns another person and forces him or her to work for no pay. Many years ago, Southern farmers kept African Americans as slaves to pick cotton and other crops on their farms. These farms were called plantations. The slaves did not have the same rights as their owners and were often mistreated.

Union: When the Southern states seceded, the Northern states became known as the Union. Union soldiers were known to wear navy blue uniforms during the Civil War.